A Song and Puzzle Book

Old MacDonald Had a Farm

Highlights Press
Honesdale, Pennsylvania

Old MacDonald had a farm. E-I-E-I-O.

What silly things do you see in the barnyard?

3

And on that farm he had a COW.
E-I-E-I-O.

Help the cow find her way to the herd.
How many sheep do you see?
What else can you count?

Illustrated by Laura Zarrin

5

With a **moo, moo** here and a **moo, moo** there.

Here a **moo**, there a **moo**.

Everywhere a **moo, moo.**

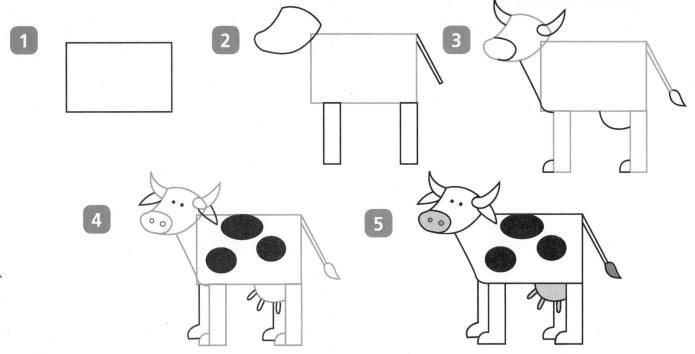

Follow the steps above to learn how to draw a cow,
or draw one from your own head.

Hidden Pictures

Can you find these 5 hidden objects?

ring

mitten

artist's brush

shoe

feather

Old MacDonald had a farm. E-I-E-I-O.

Old MacDonald had a farm. E-I-E-I-O.
And on that farm he had a pig.
E-I-E-I-O.

How many letter **P**'s do you see?

PINK LEMONADE

With an **oink, oink** here and an **oink, oink** there.
Here an **oink**, there an **oink**.
Everywhere an **oink, oink**.

Use the words to finish the poem.

skin   pool   cool   in

When it's hot the pigs keep _____,
relaxing in a muddy _____.
Running up, then jumping _____,
they slip and slop and soak their _____.

Can you find the 5 socks hidden in the picture?

Old MacDonald had a farm. E-I-E-I-O.

Illustrated by Luanne Marten

11

Old MacDonald had a farm. E-I-E-I-O.
And on that farm he had a **horse**.
E-I-E-I-O.

What silly things do you see on the trail?

Illustrated by Sean Parkes

With a **neigh, neigh** here and a **neigh, neigh** there.
Here a **neigh**, there a **neigh**.
Everywhere a **neigh, neigh**.

Follow the steps above to learn how to draw a horse,
or draw one from your own head.

Illustrated by Ron Zalme

Hidden Pictures® Can you find these 8 hidden objects?

racket

rowboat

raindrop

radish

rose

ruler

rocket

ring

Old MacDonald had a farm. E-I-E-I-O.

Old MacDonald had a farm. **E-I-E-I-O.**
And on that farm he had a **cat.**
E-I-E-I-O.

How many cats do you see?
How many flowers do you see?
What else can you count?

17

With a **meow, meow** here and a **meow, meow** there.
Here a **meow**, there a **meow**.
Everywhere a **meow, meow**.

Each kitten has an identical twin.
Can you find each pair?

Old MacDonald had a farm. E-I-E-I-O.

Help the mother cats find their kittens.

Old MacDonald had a farm. E-I-E-I-O.

How are these pictures the same?

And on that farm he had a duck. E-I-E-I-O.

How are they different?

With a **quack**, **quack** here and a **quack**, **quack** there.

Here a **quack**, there a **quack**.

Everywhere a **quack**, **quack**.

Who am I?
I'm not in the water.
I'm not on the land.
Look on the rock,
And here I stand!

How many
ducklings do
you see?

baseball
bat

cookie

fire
hydrant

cowboy
hat

ice-cream
cone

crescent
moon

palm tree

Old MacDonald had a farm. E-I-E-I-O.

Old MacDonald had a farm. E-I-E-I-O.
And on that farm he had a **dog**.
E-I-E-I-O.

What silly things do you see?

With a **woof, woof** here
and a **woof, woof** there.
Here a **woof**, there a **woof**.
Everywhere a **woof, woof**.

Look for each object in the big picture.
Write the letters you find in the blanks.

Why did the puppy jump into the water?

Because he was a ☐ ☐ ☐ ☐ ☐ ☐ !

Can you find the 5 spoons hidden in the picture?

Old MacDonald had a farm. E-I-E-I-O.

Illustrated by Deborah Melmon

27

Old MacDonald had a farm. E-I-E-I-O.
And on that farm he had a **chicken**.
E-I-E-I-O.

Each rooster has an exact match. Can you find all 10 pairs?

With a **cluck, cluck** here and a **cluck, cluck** there.
Here a **cluck,** there a **cluck.**
Everywhere a **cluck, cluck.**

Draw lines to match
the words that rhyme.

Egg	Hello
Chick	Sleep
Peep	Leg
Yellow	Sing
Wing	Quick

How many eggs did each hen lay?

Old MacDonald had a farm. E-I-E-I-O.

Illustrated by Helena Bogosian

31

Old MacDonald had a farm. E-I-E-I-O.

How are these pictures the same?

Illustrated by Dave Klug

And on that farm he had a sheep. E-I-E-I-O.

How are they different?

With a **baa, baa** here and a **baa, baa** there.
Here a **baa,** there a **baa.**
Everywhere a **baa, baa.**

Find the two sheep that look the same.

cat

mug

airplane

rug

sock

lock

mitten

cane

Old MacDonald had a farm. E-I-E-I-O.

Old MacDonald had a farm. E-I-E-I-O.
And on that farm he had a frog.
E-I-E-I-O.

How many frogs
do you see at the pond?

Can you also find
6 dragonflies?

Illustrated by Paul Sharp

With a **ribbit, ribbit** here and a **ribbit, ribbit** there.
Here a **ribbit,** there a **ribbit.**
Everywhere a **ribbit, ribbit.**

Illustrated by Ron Zalme

1

2

3

4

5

Follow the steps above to learn how to draw a frog,
or draw one from your own head.

Hidden Pictures® Can you find these 8 hidden objects?

crescent moon

crayon

spoon

baseball

saltshaker

pizza

ladder

banana

Old MacDonald had a farm . . .

Horse

Sheep

Goose

Cat

Dog

Duck

Pig

Chicken

Goat

Cow

Every mama on the left has a baby on the right.
Find all 10 matching pairs.

Calf

Chick

Kitten

Puppy

Gosling

Kid

Duckling

Piglet

Lamb

Foal

E-I-E-I-O!

Illustrated by John Courtney

How are these pictures the same?

How are they different?

Can you find each of these animals in the book?

Chicken

Cow

Pig

Duck

Cat

Horse

Sheep

Frog

Dog

What is your favorite farm animal?
Draw it here.

Illustrated by Jack Desrocher

Answers

PAGES 4–5

PAGE 7

PAGES 8–9

PAGE 10

When it's hot the pigs keep __cool__,
relaxing in a muddy __pool__.
Running up, then jumping __in__,
they slip and slop and soak their __skin__.

PAGE 11

PAGE 15

PAGE 18

Answers

PAGE 19

PAGES 20–21

PAGE 22

PAGE 23

PAGE 26

Why did the puppy jump
into the water?

Because he was a
hot dog!

PAGE 27

PAGES 28–29

PAGE 30

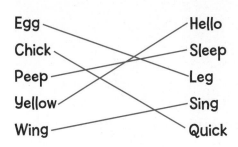

Egg ——— Leg
Chick ——— Quick
Peep ——— Sleep
Yellow ——— Hello
Wing ——— Sing

Answers

PAGE 31

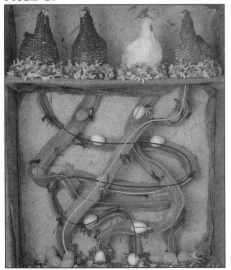

PAGES 32–33

PAGE 34

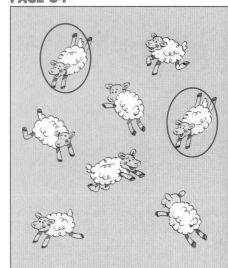

PAGE 35

PAGES 36–37

PAGE 39

PAGES 40–41